George A. Leavitt

Valuable paintings

George A. Leavitt

Valuable paintings

ISBN/EAN: 9783742866974

Manufactured in Europe, USA, Canada, Australia, Japa

Cover: Foto ©Thomas Meinert / pixelio.de

Manufactured and distributed by brebook publishing software
(www.brebook.com)

George A. Leavitt

Valuable paintings

No. 165.   *Meissonier.*

HALT AT A CABARET.

VALUABLE PAINTINGS.

THE COLLECTIONS OF

MR. JOHN H. SHERWOOD AND MR. BENJ. HART,

NOW ON EXHIBITION AT THE

Ṅational Academy of Ḍesign,

CORNER OF 23d STREET AND 4th AVENUE,

AND

WILL BE SOLD AT AUCTION

AT

CHICKERING HALL,

WEDNESDAY AND THURSDAY EVENINGS,

December 17th and 18th, 1879.

GEO. A. LEAVITT & CO.   R. SOMERVILLE, *Auctioneer.*

⁎⁎ Under the direction of S. P. AVERY. *⁎⁎*

THIS SALE WILL TAKE PLACE AT CHICKERING HALL, ON
WEDNESDAY AND THURSDAY EVE'GS, DEC. 17 AND 18.

CONDITIONS OF SALE.

1. *The highest Bidder to be the Buyer, and if any dispute arise between two or more Bidders, the Lot so in dispute shall be immediately put up again and re-sold.*

2. *The Purchasers to give their names and addresses, and to pay down twenty-five per cent. on the dollar in part payment, or the whole of the Purchase-money, if required, in default of which the Lot or Lots so purchased to be immediately put up again and re-sold.*

3. *The Lots to be taken away at the Buyer's Expense and Risk within three days from the conclusion of the Sale, and the remainder of the Purchase-money to be absolutely paid, or otherwise settled for to the satisfaction of the Vendors, on or before delivery: in default of which Messrs.* GEO. A. LEAVITT & CO. *will not hold themselves responsible, if the Lots be lost, stolen, damaged, or destroyed, but they will be left at the sole risk of the Purchaser.*

4. *The Sale of any Painting, Engraving, Print, Furniture, Works of Art, or any other article, is not to be set aside on account of any error in the description. All articles are exposed for Public Exhibition one or more days, and are sold just as they are without recourse.*

5. *To prevent inaccuracy in delivery and inconvenience in the settlement of the Purchases, no Lot can, on any account be removed during the Sale.*

6. *Upon failure of complying with the above conditions, the money deposited in part payment shall be forfeited; all Lots uncleared within the time aforesaid shall be re-sold by public or private Sale, without further notice, and the deficiency (i* any) attending such re-sale, shall be made good by the Defaulter at this Sale, together with all charges attending the same. This Condition is without prejudice to the right of the Auctioneers to enforce the contract made at this Sale, without such re-sale, if they think fit.*

GEO. A. LEAVITT & CO.

Mr. S. P. Avery respectfully announces that he has been authorized by Messrs. John H. Sherwood and Benjamin Hart to sell at public auction their valuable collections of paintings, by noted American and Foreign artists.

They will be on exhibition at the galleries of the " National Academy of Design," corner of 23d Street and 4th Avenue, from Saturday, December 6th, until Wednesday, December 17th (inclusive). They will be sold at Chickering Hall, by R. Somerville, auctioneer, on Wednesday and Thursday evenings, December 17th and 18th. The importance of these collections will make the sale second (only) in value in the history of art-auctions in this country.

Mr. Sherwood's collection has been made familiar in many generous ways, and he has been long and favorably known for his efforts in behalf of art, and for his liberal patronage of our home school. Nearly all of his pictures, by American, English, and Scotch artists, were painted expressly to his order, and many are the master-pieces of their authors.

Mr. Hart's collection is composed entirely of works by foreign artists of distinction in the different schools, collected by him during several years of residence abroad, with great taste, care, and cost, and under most favorable intercourse with the artists, and having been rarely seen out of his house in Madison Avenue, they will have the charm of novelty.

Mr. Sherwood not being a housekeeper, and Mr. Hart intending in future to reside abroad, are the reasons for the disposal of these choice collections. Not a single painting has been withheld, nothing has been added ; the word of these gentlemen has been pledged that not one shall be bought in, and Mr. Avery is charged to see that this pledge will be strictly carried out.

₊ The sale will be under the supervision of S. P. Avery, of No. 86 Fifth Avenue, to whom orders to purchase and other communications may be addressed.*₊*

NAMES OF THE 114 ARTISTS REPRESENTED IN THIS CATALOGUE.

ACHENBACH, 129.
BAUGNIET, 27.
BAKKERKORFF, 98.
BELLANGE, 101.
BEARNARD, 43.
BILLOTTE, 83.
BOULANGER, 161.
BOUDIN, 21.
BONHEUR, 31, 123.
BOUTIBONNE, 106.
CARLINI, 3, 81.
CABANEL, 120.
CHAPLIN, 29.
CHAVET, 97.
CHARNAY, 94.
CLAYS, 131.
COUTOURIER, 34.
COL (DAVID), 59.
COROT, 76, 153, 162.
DAUBIGNY, 55.
DE DREUX, 26.
DECAMPS, 155.
DE KEYSER, 21.

DETAILLE, 67.
DE NITTIS, 23, 119.
DIAZ, 71, 159.
DURAN, 75.
DUPRE, 77, 103.
DUVERGER, 9, 88.
DRUMMOND, 39, 135.
ESCOSURA, 65.
FORTUNY, 20, 104.
FLUGGEN, 42.
GESLER, 14.
GAUERMANN, 140.
GEROME, 160.
GESSA, 113.
GIRARD, 112.
GLAIZE, 63, 138.
GOUPIL, 35.
GUES, 73.
HEILBUTH, 66.
HERBSTOFFER, 99.
HERDMANN, 132.
MILLEMACHER, 32.
JACQUE, 72, 108.

JACQUET, 74.
JAZET, 122.
JIMINEZ, 25.
JONGKIND, 8, 87.
KNAUS, 79.
KOLLER, 64.
KOWALSKI, 96.
LAMBINET, 17.
LE POITTEVIN, 110.
MADRAZO, 38, 146.
MAGNUS, 10.
MEISSONIER, 165.
MELIN, 50.
MICHETTI, 155.
MULREADY, 85.
OMMEGANCK, 22.
PALMAROLI, 144.
PARITICELLI, 93.
PELOUZE, 12.
PILLE, 44.
PLASSAN, 95.
RICO, 41, 116, 149.
ROYBET, 53, 147.

ROUSSEAU, 78.
ROSSI, 164.
ROTTA, 143.
SCHREYER, 58, 134.
SCHENCK, 15.
SCHREBER, 86.
SEIGNAC, 91.
SORDET, 1, 84.
STEELL, 13, 45, 103, 136, 157.
STAMMEL, 48.
STEVENS, 158.
TROVON, 62, 80, 156, 163.
VAN MARCKE, 60, 128.
VAN MIERIS, 145.
VERNON, 16, 124.
VILLEGAS, 137.
VIRY, 154.
VIBERT, 69, 107.
VOLLON, 28.
WORMS, 56.
ZAMACOIS, 70, 152.
ZIEM, 47, 128.
ZIMMERMANN, 151.

BY AMERICAN ARTISTS.

BROWN (J. G.), 57, 105, 139.
BROWN (W. M.), 6.
BOUGHTON, 18, 68, 114.
COLMAN, 111.
DOUGHTY, 51.
GIFFORD (S. R.), 90, 100.
GIFFORD (SWAYNE), 30.
GUY (S. J.), 4, 36, 54, 92, 142.

GUY (MISS), 2, 82.
HART (J. M.), 52.
HOMER, 40, 49, 121.
IRVING, 24, 115.
KENSETT, 130.
LAY, 37.
MORGAN, 109.
RICHARDS, 33, 141.

SONNTAG, 46, 150.
SHATTUCK, 19.
SCOTT, 5.
SARGENT, 61.
WARD, 117.
WHITTREDGE, 143.
WYANT, 148.

CATALOGUE.

The first figure indicates the WIDTH of each picture.

— —

I

SORDET (E.)   .   .   .   .   Geneva

Pupil of Calame.

SWISS LANDSCAPE.

10 x 7

2

GUY (Miss)   .   .   .   New York.

FRUIT.

10 x 8

3

CARLINI (Guelio) . . . . Venice.

THE ABDUCTION.

Water-Color.

9 x 10

4

GUY (S. J.), N. A. . . . New York.

BLACK HAMBURG GRAPES.

12 x 16

5

SCOTT (Julian). N. A. . New York.

THE CAPTURED RECORDS.

10 x 12

6

BROWN (W. M.) . . . New York.

FRUIT.

8 x 10

No. 28. *Vollon.*

THE SEINE AT BERCEY.

7

AFTER HOLBEIN.

Miniatures in ivory.   In frames of bronze.

EARL OF ORMOND (father of Anne Boleyn).
SIR THOMAS WYAT.

3½ x 4½

8

JONGKIND (J. B.) . . . . Paris.

Pupil of Isabey.
Medal 1852.

MOONLIGHT.

8 x 10

9

DUVERGER (T. E.) . . . Paris.

Medals, 1861, '63, '65.

THE MORAL OF THE BOTTLE.

16 x 19

10

MAGNUS . . . . Paris.

Pupil of Diaz.

A CLEARING IN THE FOREST.

23 x 18

No. 30. Gifford.

NEAR THE LANDING PLACE.

664.

50.

11 *J. J. Drake*
546. mad. ave. Paris.

BOUDIN (E.) .

TROUVILLE.

15 x 8

12 *a. c. whitney*

PELOUSE (L. G.) . . . . Paris.

180.

Medals, 1873, '76.
Medal Exposition Universelle, 1878.
Legion of Honor, 1878.

VILLAGE OF CERNAY.

21 x 12

13 *W. Watson*

STEELL (Gourlay), R.S.A. *59. Wall St.* Edinburgh.
60. Animal painter to the Queen in Scotland.

THE TEMPORARY SHADE.

14 x 20

14 *W. P. Ward* Munich.

GEBLER (F. Otto) .

N. Medal, Berlin, 1874. *174. Duane*
THE SHADOW.

12 x 9

1.034

No. 33. Richard.   AUTUMN.

1.034.

360.

15 *a. R. Whitney*

SCHENCK (A. F.) . . . . Paris.

Pupil of Cogniet.
Medal, 1865.
Chevalier of the Order of Christ of Portugal, and of Isabel the
Catholic.

SHEEP IN A SNOW-STORM.

23 x 15

16 *D. Cole*

55.

VERNON (A. I.) . . . . London.

AN ENGLISH PARK.

24 x 15

17 *mr. Bell*
Brevoort House

LAMBINET (E.), dec'd. . Paris.

260.

Medals, 1843, '53, '57.
Legion of Honor, 1867.
Born, 1810. Died, 1878.

LANDSCAPE.

17 x 13

18 *a. R. Whitney*

BOUGHTON (Geo. H.), N.A. and A.R.A. London.

550.

BURNING FAGGOTS.

13¼ x 9¼

2,259

No. 43. Barnard.

GOING TO THE DANCE.

SHATTUCK (A. D.), N. A. New York.

19

SHEEP AND CATTLE.

24 x 16

[handwritten: 2.259.]
[handwritten: 185]
[handwritten: J. W. Wheele.]
[handwritten: 25. W. 19]

20

FORTUNY (Mariano), dec'd. Rome.

Pupil of the Barcelona Academy.
Chevalier of the Order of Charles III.
Prize of Rome, from Spain, 1858.
Diploma to the memory of deceased artists.
Exposition Universelle, 1878.
Born, 1838. Died, 1874.

A SPANISH LADY.

Water-Color.

10 x 14

[handwritten: 110.]

21

DE KEYSER (N.) Antwerp.

Pupil of the Antwerp Academy.
Medals, 1836, '40.
Chevalier of the Order of Leopold, and of the Lion of the Netherlands.
President of the Academy of Antwerp.

A SCHOLAR OF THE MIDDLE AGES.

12 x 14

[handwritten: 100.]
[handwritten: J. a. Coale fr.]
[handwritten: St. Louis]

[handwritten: 2).6574]

No. 45. Steell.

DEER STALKING.

2.654 *Bell*

22

OMMEGANCK (deceased).

170.   *THE SHEPHERD'S REPOSE.*

19 x 15

23

DE NITTIS (J.)   .   .   .   .   Paris.

450.
Pupil of Gérome.
Medal, 1876.
Medal, Exposition Universelle, 1878.
Legion of Honor, 1878.

THE QUARREL.

6 x 9

24 *C. P. Huntington*

IRVING (J. B.), N. A., dec'd,   .   New York.

560.   Born, 1826. Died, 1877.

THE CONNOISSEURS.—Statue of Venus de Medici.

14 x 12

25 *W. L. Fraser*

JIMINEZ (Prieto M.)   *148.e.* 30 Rome.

330   *SERVANTS' HALL IN THE ALHAMBRA.*

14 x 18

4.164

No. 62. *Hart (J. M.)* UNDER THE BOUGHS.

4.164

18~~5~~.

DE DREUX (Alfred) 26 *William Everett* *Boston* . Paris.

Pupil of L. Cogniet.
Medals, 1834, '44, '48.
Legion of Honor, 1857.
Born, 1812. Died, 1860.

A FOX CHASE.

21 x 15

BAUGNIET (Charles) 27 *B. B. Knight* *Providence* aris.

33 0.

Pupil of Drolling.
Medals, 1865 ; Vienna, 1873.
Chevalier of the Order of Leopold of Belgium, of Isabel the
Catholic, of Christ of Portugal, and of the
Branche Ernestine de Saxe.

WAITING FOR THE OPERA.

17 x 21

VOLLON (A.) 28 *P. Van Volkenburgh* . Paris.

410.

Pupil of the Academy at Lyons.
Medals, 1865, '68, '69.
Legion of Honor, 1870.
Medal, Exposition Universelle, 1878.
Officer of the Legion of Honor, 1878.

THE SEINE AT BERCEY.

16 x 8

5.089.

No. 55. Danbigny.

AUTMN AT AUVERS.

5089

CHAPLIN (C.)   29 *Knoedler & Co*   .   .   .   Paris.

200.

Pupil of Drolling.
Medals, 1851, '52, '65.
Legion of Honor, 1865.
Officer of the Legion of Honor, 1877.

A STUDY OF GEOGRAPHY.

7 x 12

30 *A. R. Whitney*

GIFFORD (R Swayne), N. A. .   .   New York.

230.   *NEAR THE LANDING-PLACE—OCTOBER.*

26 x 15

31 *A. Kohn*

BONHEUR (J. Peyrol)   .   Paris.

Pupil of her sister.

410.   *ANIMALS IN PASTURE.*

25 x 17

5929

No. 68. Hailbach. THE PROMENADE.

J. 929.

HILLEMACHER (E.) [32] *a. R. whitney* . . . Paris.

600.

Pupil of L. Cogniet.
Medals, 1848, '57, '61, '63.
Legion of Honor, 1865.

THE MARIONETTES.

25 x 19

RICHARDS (Wm. T.) [33] *a. l. whitney* . Philadelphia.

375.

PARADISE POINT, NEWPORT—AUTUMN.

20 x 24

COUTURIER (P. L.) [34] *L. a. Couturier* . . . Paris.

100.

Pupil of Picot.
Medals, 1855, '61.

A FRENCH BARN-YARD.

No. 66. Detaille. INCROYABLES.

7.004

35 *a.R. Whitney*

GOUPIL (Jules) . . . Paris.

Pupil of A. Scheffer.
Medals, 1873, '74, '75.
Medal, Exposition Universelle, 1878.

250.

THE DUET.

25 x 31

36 *E. N. Dickerson*
6 it. C. 34

GUY (S. J.), N. A. . . . New York.

1.225,

BABY'S BEDTIME.

24 x 32

37 *D. Cole*

LAY (Oliver), A. N. A. . . . New York.

190.

THE TWO FRIENDS.

32 x 24

38 *Knoedler bo.*

MADRAZO (R. de) . . . Paris.

Pupil of his father.
Legion of Honor, 1878.
Medal, Exposition Universelle, 1878.

900.

BAL-MASQUE, "VALENTINO."

31 x 19

9.569.

No. 75.   Carolus—Duran.   ORIENTAL WOMAN.

9.569

DRUMMOND (Jas.), R. S. A. 39 *Mariner Windsor Hotel* . Edinburgh.

27 5

CROMBIE'S CLOSE.
. *SIR WALTER SCOTT AT THE BRIC-A-BRAC SHOP*
OF JOHN HOWELL.

25 × 35

John Howell was a noted character, a lovable, quaint, picturesque old man, who died only a few years ago in Edinburgh. He called himself a poly-artist; he was a dealer in curiosities, also was a collector of old ballads, and a man of some scholarship, among other things having written the best treatise upon Roman galleys. He was frequently visited by Sir Walter Scott, who had much in common with the old man, and for whom he had great respect.

40 *a. R. Whitney*

HOMER (Winslow). N. A. . New York.

A COUNTRY SCHOOL-ROOM IN THE CATSKILLS.

420.

38 × 21

41 *H. R. Bishop*

RICO (M. D.) . . . New York. . Paris.

Pupil of Madrazo.
Medal, Exposition Universelle, 1873.
Legion of Honor, 1878.

NEAR BOUGIVAL.

775

35 × 19

11.039

No. 11. Dupré.

LANDSCAPE.

11.039.

42 *a. f. whitney*

FLUGGEN (Gisbert), dec'd. . . Munich.

310. *THE INTERRUPTED MARRIAGE CONTRACT.*

36 x 27

43 *B. B. Knight*

BEARNARD (F.) . . . London.

Exhibited at Royal Academy, London, 1873.

420. *GOING TO THE DANCE IN OLD ENGLAND.*

36 x 24

44 *J. J. Drake*

PILLE (C. H.) . . . Paris.

Pupil of F. Barrias.
Medals, 1869, '72.

560.

AUTUMN.

34 x 45

45 *B. B. Knight*

STEELL (Gourlay) . . . Edinburgh.

Animal painter to the Queen in Scotland.

300. *DEER STALKING—HIGHLANDS.*

41 x 32

12.634

No. 78. Rousseau.

HAMLET OF BERRI.

12.634.

46 *Jas Buell*

SONNTAG (W. L.), N. A. . . New York.

500. *AUTUMN—WHITE MOUNTAINS.*

54 x 33

47 *L. A. Lautrier*

ZIEM (Felix) . . . Paris.

Medals, 1851, '52, '55.
Legion of Honor, 1857.

800. *GARDEN AT VENICE.*

49 x 32

48 *C. Victor*

STAMMEL (E.) . . Düsseldorf.

310. *ARMORER'S SHOP.*

36 x 28

49 *A. L. Whitney*

HOMER (Winslow), N. A. . . New York.

290. *WEANING THE CALF.*

38 x 24

14.534.

No. 70. Knaus. THE "BEE FATHER."

14.534

MELIN (J.) . 50 *L. Dohest 322. mad. ave* . Paris.

Pupil of P. Delaroche.
Medals, 1843, '45, '55, '58.

2OO.

"DEAD FOR A DUCAT."

32 x 24

GIFFORD (S. R.), N. A. 50 a *S. M. Vose Providence* New York.

210.

VILLA MALTA.

13 x 26

DOUGHTY (Thos.), N. A., dec'd. 51 *Welch Grosvenor House* New York.

155.

Born, 1793. Died, 1856.

CATSKILL MOUNTAINS—FROM SAUGERTIES.

36 x 28

HART (J. M.), N. A . 52 *A. R. Whitney* . New York,

390.

UNDER THE BOUGHS.

34 x 24

15.489

No. 80. Troyon.

COW AND DOG.

15.489

ROYBET (F.)   .   53   *J. C. Runkle*   .   Paris.

Medal, 18**6**.

525

DEATH OF ROXANA.

29 x 25

The scene reproduced by the artist was suggested by Racine's Tragedy. Bajazet was brother of Amurat, 4th Sultan of the Turkish Empire, who ascended the throne 1623. This sovereign had designated from among his wives, Roxana, to bear the title of Sultana; this lady forgot the debt of gratitude she owed to him who had preferred her to her rivals, in abandoning herself without scruples to the passion she felt awakening in her heart for Bajazet. She was in possession of an order for his death, that Amurat had confided to her prior to his departure for the conquest of Babylonia. Roxana did not long hide from the knowledge of this prince the power with which she was clothed, and, furthermore, offered to aid him to usurp the throne, if he would put himself at the head of a revolt, which would result in the death of Amurat, on condition he would marry her. Bajazet had long loved Attalida, his cousin, an obscure personage at the imperial court. Roxana, annoyed by the repeated refusals of Bajazet, ordered his assassination; she herself was soon put to death by a messenger sent by Amurat, who had been secretly informed of her projects of treason toward her master.

GUY (S. J.), N. A.   .   54   *J. Buell*   .   New York.

475.

ONE TOO MANY.

30 x 25

16.489

No. 102. *Jacque.*

SHEEP AND LAMB

16.489.

55 *Knoedler & Co.*

DAUBIGNY (C. F.), dec'd. . . . Paris.

500.

Pupil of P. Delaroche.
Medals, 1848, '53, '55, '57, '59, '67.
Legion of Honor, 1859.
Officer of the Legion of Honor, 1874.
Diploma to the Memory of Deceased Artists.
Exposition Universelle, 1878.
Born, 1817.   Died, 1878.

AUTUMN AT AUVERS.

32 x 18

56 *Russell*

WORMS (Jules) . . . Paris.

220.

Pupil of Lafosse.
Medals, 1867, '68, '69.
Legion of Honor, 1876.
Medal, Exposition Universelle, 1878.

SMUGGLERS OF LA RONDA.

16 x 21

57 *William Everett*

BROWN (J. G.), N. A. . . . New York.

150

THE RELUCTANT BRIDE.

20 x 27

17.359

No. 104. *Fortuny.*   THE MODEL.

17.309

William Everett

SCHREYER (AD.) . . . . Paris.

1.125

Medals, 1864, '65, (E. U.) '67.
Vienna Exposition, 1873.

WALLACHIANS RECONNOITERING.

28 x 16

59 *N. H. Webb.*

COL (David) . . . . Antwerp.

500.

Pupil of De Keyser.
Medal, Vienna Exposition, 1873.
Chevalier of the Order of Leopold.

THE WINE-TASTERS.

14 x 18

of Van Volkenburgh

VAN MARCKE (E.) . . Paris.

925.

Pupil of Troyon.
Medals, 1867, '69, '70.
Legion of Honor, 1872.
Medal at Exposition Universelle, 1878.

PASTURAGE IN THE LANDES.

26 x 18

19.909

No. 105.   J. G. Brown.

WINTER SPORTS.

19.909.

SARGENT (J. S.) . 61 *Mr. Lichtenauer* . 139. IV. 44. . Paris.

160.

Pupil of C. Duran.
Honorable Mention, Salon, 1879.

THE LUXEMBOURG GARDENS.

TROYON (Constant), dec'd. 62 *J. P. A.* . Paris.

460.

Pupil of Rivereux.
Medals, 1838, '40, '46, '48, '55.
Legion of Honor, 1849.
Born, 1810. Died, 1865.

THE FORD.

13 x 9

GLAIZE (Léon) . 63 *G. H. Peabody* . Paris.

300.

Pupil of Gérome.
Medals, 1864, '66, '68.
Legion of Honor, 1877.
Medal, Exposition Universelle, 1878.

POMPEIAN IMAGE-SELLER.

19 x 13

20.829

No. 111.   *Colman.*   Tower of the Giralda.

20.829

64 *a. l. Whitney*

KOLLER (G.) . . . Brussels.

3/6.

Pupil of the Academy of Vienna.
Medal, Vienna, 1873.
Paris Universal Exposition, 1878.

MARRIAGE OF THE ARCHDUKE OF AUSTRIA TO
PHILLOPENA WELSLER.

12 x 14

65 *Mr. Bell.*

ESCOSURA (Léon) . . Paris.

4 50.

Pulpil of Gérome.
Commander of the Order of Isabel the Catholic.
Chevalier of the Order of Charles III. of Spain.
Chevalier of the Order of Christ of Portugal.

A CAVALIER.

7¼ x 10¼

66 *Knoedler &o.*

HEILBUTH (F.) . Paris.

330.

Pupil of
Medals, 1857, '59, '61.
Legion of Honor, 1861.

THE PROMENADE.

No. 112. *Girard.*   ARCADIA.

21.984

DETAILLE (E.) .   67 *J. C. Runkle* .   . Paris.

950.

Pupil of E. Meissonier.
Medals, 1869, '70, '72.
Legion of Honor, 1873.

INCROYABLES.

6 x 8

68 *P. Van Volkenburgh*

BOUGHTON (Geo. H.), N. A. .   . London.

Associate of Royal Academy.

260.   *MOONLIGHT SKATING SCENE.*

12 x 7

69 *H. R. Bishop*

VIBERT (J. G.) .   . Paris.

1.600

Pupil of Barrias.
Medals, 1864, '67, '68.
Legion of Honor, 1870.
Medal at Exposition Universelle, 1878.

*SPANISH MATADOR PREPARING FOR A BULL-
FIGHT.*

9 x 13

24.794

No. 114. *Boughton.*

WOUTER VAN TWILLER.

24,794

ZAMACOIS (Edouard), dec'd. 70 *H.C. Durant* *117. E. 57* . Paris.

250.

Pupil of Meissonier.
Medal, 1867.
Diploma to the memory of deceased artists.
Exposition Universelle, 1878.
Born, 1843.   Died, 1871.

WAITING.

4 x 6

DIAZ (N.), dec'd. 71 *J. P. a.* . Paris.

260.

Medals, 1844, '46, '48.
Legion of Honor, 1851.
Diploma to the memory of deceased artists.
Exposition Universelle, 1878.
Born, 1807.   Died, 1876.

A WOOD SCENE.

10½ x 13½

JACQUE (Charles) 72 *H. C. Bishop* . Paris.

300.

Medals, 1861, '63, '64.
Legion of Honor, 1867.

POULTRY.

15 x 8

25,604

No. 115. *Irving.*

THE END OF THE GAME.

GUES (Alfred) . . Paris.

Pupil of

460. *BOCCACCIO RECITING HIS POEMS.*

Costume of the 14th Century.

14 X 11

74 *J. Dunlap*

JACQUET (J. G.) . . Paris.

200. Pupil of Bouguereau.
Medals, 1868, '75.
Medal, Exposition Universelle, 1878.

A LESSON IN SHOOTING.

11 x 16

75 *Knoedler &o.*

DURAN (Carolus) . . . Paris.

630. Pupil of Souchon.
Medals, 1866, '69, '70.
Legion of Honor, 1872.
Medal, Exposition Universelle, 1878.
Officer of the Legion of Honor, 1878.
Grand Medal of Honor, 1879.

ORIENTAL WOMAN.

14 x 25

26.894.

No. 110. *Rice.*

NEAR POISSY, ON THE SEINE.

26.894

COROT (J. B. C.), dec'd . . Paris.

320

Pupil of V. Bertin.
Medals, 1838, '48, '55, '67 (E. U.)
Legion of Honor, 1846.
Officer of the Legion of Honor, 1867.
Diploma to the memory of deceased artists.
Exposition Universelle, 1878.
Born, 1796. Died, 1875.

THE SEINE AT BEZONS.

18 x 21

77 *J. T. Kroat*

DUPRÉ (Jules) . . . . . Paris

900.

Medals, 1833 (E. U.), '67.
Legion of Honor, 1849.
Officer of the Legion of Honor, 1870.

LANDSCAPE.

19 x 12.

H. G. Marquand

78

ROUSSEAU (Theo.), dec'd. . . Paris.

1.125

Pupil of Lethiere.
Medals, 1834, '49, '55.
Legion of Honor, 1867.
One of the Eight Grand Medals of Honor (E. U.), 1867.
Diploma to the memory of deceased artists.
Exposition Universelle, 1878.
Born, 1812. Died, 1867.

THE HAMLET OF BERRI.

No. 118. *Ziem.*

END OF THE GRAND CANAL.

29.339

KNAUS (I..), Prof. *M. H. Sandford Lexington Ky* . Berlin.

3.900

Pupil of the Dusseldorf Academy.
Medals, 1853–55 (E. U.), 1857–59.
Legion of Honor, 1859.
Grand Medal of Honor (E. U.), 1867.
Officer of the Legion of Honor, 1867.
Professor in the Academy, Berlin.

THE "BEE FATHER."

15 x 19

80 *J. R. Butter,*

TROYON (C.), dec'd. . . . Paris.

1.725

Pupil of Rivereux.
Medals, 1838, '40, '46, '48, '55.
Legion of Honor, 1849.
Born, 1810.   Died, 1865.

COW AND DOG.

25 x 20

ALX CABANEL

No. 120. Cabanel.

EVE, AFTER THE FALL

34.264

THURSDAY, DECEMBER 18TH,

AT HALF-PAST SEVEN O'CLOCK.

25.   81   *A. Van Santvoord*

CARLINI (Guelio)   .   .   .   Venice.

VENETIAN SERENADERS.

Water-Color.

8 x 12

                82   *Friedman*
                     3. Pine st.

GUY (Miss)   .   .   .   .   New York.

30.   *FRUIT IN SILVER BASKET.*

13 x 9

                83   *C. F. Hasseltine*
                     Phila
                          Paris.

BILLOTTE (L. J.)   .   .   .   Paris.

Pupil of Blondel.

30.   *CLASPING THE GIRDLE.*

8 x 10

34.349

No. 121. Homer.

SNAPPING THE WHIP.

34.349.

SORDET (E.) .   .   . **84** *C. J. Wolff*

Geneva.

Pupil of Calame.   *65. E. 55.*

30.

SWISS LAKE.

10 x 7

85 *R. J. Fryoat*

MULREADY (A. E.) .   .   . London.

80.

WITHOUT A HOME.

4 x 6½

86 *H. Q. Robinson*

SCHEERES

I. E. 27. Hague.

35.

TESTING THE SWORD.

6 x 7

87 *W. P. Ward*

JONGKIND (J. B.) .   .   . *174. Duane St.* Paris.

Pupil of Isabey.
Medal, 1852.

55.

SUNSET—HOLLAND.

8 x 10

No. 125. *Decamps.*　　　　　　EASTERN SLAVE MARKET.

34. 5 4 9

135.

DUVERGER (T. E.) . 88 *L. A. Lanthier* . . . Paris.

Medals, 1861, '63, '65

BAD NEWS.

10 X 13

27.

AFTER HOLBEIN. 89 *Jms Pondir*

Miniatures in ivory, in frames of bronze.

SIR THOMAS MORE. *da*

90

MRS. DAUNSEY—2d daughter of Sir Thomas More.

3½ X 4½

27.

SEIGNAC (P.) . 91 *D. Q. Lyall* *Wall* *st.* . Paris.

110.

Pupil of Picot.

90. *EMBROIDERING.*

8½ X 10½

GUY (S. J.), N. A. 92 *J. Y. Johnston* . New York.

80.

PORTRAIT OF C. L. ELLIOTT.

10 X 12

34.908

No. 127. *Guy.* MOTHER'S SUPPLICATION.

34.908

93 *G. H. Peabody*

PARITICELLI . . Rome.

5/5.

INVESTIGATION.

8 x 11

94 *H. I. Ord.*

CHARNAY (A.) . . . . Paris.

190.

Pupil of Pils.
Medal, 1876.

GIRL PICKING FLOWERS.

8 x 6

95 *Jos. Tondir.*

PLASSAN (A. E.) . . . Paris.

Medals, 1852, '57, '59.
Legion of Honor, 1859.

190.

THE REPAST.

5 x 4

96 *P. Van Volkenburgh*

KOWALSKI (A. W.) . . . Munich.

Pupil of Jos. Brandt.

410.

HARE HUNTING—POLAND.

11 x 17

36.273

No. 129. *Van Marcke.*   NEAR BORDEAUX.

36.2/3

CHAVET (J. V.) 97 *E. A. Wisker* . . Paris.

90.

Pupil of Revoil.
Medals, 1853, '55, '57.
Legion of Honor, 1859.

FEEDING CHICKENS.

14 x 16

BAKKERKORFF (A. H.) 98 *H. P. Bishop* . . Harlem.

Pupil of Vander Berg.

130.

TAKING HER COMFORT.

7 x 8

HERBSTHOFFER (Chas.), dec'd. . 99 *B. B. Knight* . Paris.

Medal at Vienna, 1873.

165.

THE IMPENDING CONFLICT.

9 x 6

GIFFORD (S. R.), N. A. 100 *H. P. Bishop* . . New York.

260.

FALLS OF TIVOLI.

13 x 7

No. 131. *Clays.*

HARBOR—DUTCH COAST.

36.918

101

BELLANGÉ (J. I. H.), dec'd. . . Paris.

160.

Pupil of Gros.
Medals, 1824, '55.
Legion of Honor, 1834.
Officer of the Legion of Honor, 1861.
Born, 1800. Died, 1866.

BATTLE OF SOLFERINO.

8 x 6

102

JACQUE (Charles) . . Paris.

570.

Medals, 1861, '63, '64.
Legion of Honor, 1867.

SHEEP AND LAMB.

18 x 14

103

DUPRÉ (Jules) . . Paris.

450.

Medals, 1833 (E. U.), '67.
Legion of Honor, 1849.
Officer of the Legion of Honor, 1870.

A MARSH.

15 x 18

38.038.

No. 184. *Schreyer.*

CARAVAN AT REST.

38.038

104   *C. F. Haseltine*

FORTUNY (Mariano), dec'd.   . Rome.

210.

Pupil of the Barcelona Academy.
Chevalier of the Order of Charles III.
Prize of Rome, from Spain, 1858.
Diploma to the memory of deceased artists.
Exposition Universelle, 1878.
Born, 1838. Died, 1874.

THE MODEL.

Water-Color.

9 x 13   *J. Buell*

105

BROWN (J. G.), N. A.   .   New York.

600.   *WINTER SPORTS.*

22 x 16

106   *A. T. Frost*

BOUTIBONNE (C. E.)   .   .   . Paris.

220.

Pupil of Winterhalter.
Medal, 1867.

RETURN FROM THE PROMENADE.

13 x 19

No. 113. *Rüla.*

THE VETERANS.

39.068

VIBERT (J. G.)   . *H. R. Bishop.* . Paris.

107

Pupil of Barrias.
Medals, 1854, '67, '68.
Legion of Honor, 1870.
Exposition Universelle, 1878.

THE HOUR OF THE NIGHT.

12 x 20

630.

108   *Walter*

STEELL (Gourlay), R. S. A.   .   Edinburgh.

Animal painter to the Queen in Scotland.

HIGHLAND CATTLE.

14 x 20

60.

109   *N. A. Wheelock*

MORGAN (Wm.), N. A. .   .   . New York

THE TIRED ORGAN-GRINDER.

23 x 18

175.

39.933.

No. 144. *Palmaroli.* THE MODEL.

59.933

230.

110   *D. R. Barker*

LE POITTEVIN (E.), dec'd.   .   .   Paris.

Pupil of Hersent.
Medals, 1831, '36, '48, '55
Chevalier of the Order of Leopold.
Legion of Honor, 1843.
Born, 1806.   Died, 1870.

THE WRECK.

21 x 17

L. a. Landier

111

COLMAN (S.), N. A.   .   .   .   New York.

*CORPUS CHRISTUS DAY, SEVILLE.   TOWER OF
THE GIRALDA.*

270.

19 x 29

The Giralda (so called from its vane, *que gira*, turns round; is
the finest specimen of pure Saracenic architecture in existence)
was the Meuddin tower of the adjoining mosque used to call the
faithful to prayer.   It was built in 1195, by Abur Yusef Yacub.
The foundation is made of destroyed Roman and Christian stat-
uary, the rest of a light-colored brick.   The Moorish part was
250 feet high; the upper part of 100 feet was added by Fernando
Ruis, 1568.   The vane in the pinnacle, the figure of Faith, is the
marvel of all Spaniards, as it weighs 2,800 pounds, and turns
with the slightest wind.   The tower is 50 feet square, and, seen
from a distance, is the most imposing object in Seville.

112   *B. C. Green   mad. ave
927.*   Paris.

GIRARD (Firman)   .   .   .   Paris.

Pupil of Gleyre.
Medals, 1863, '74.

ARCADIAN SCENE.

19 x 23

650.

41.088

No. 146.   *Madrazo.*   A Spanish Dance.

41,088

113 *Jno. Tondis.*

GESSA (Sebastian) . . . . Paris.

Pupil of Cabanel.

90. *STILL LIFE.*

23 x 21

114 *J. Buell.*

BOUGHTON (Geo. H.), N. A. . London.

850. Associate Member of Royal Academy.

WOUTER VAN TWILLER'S FIRST COURT IN NEW AMSTERDAM.

30 x 24

" The two parties being confronted before him, each produced a book of accounts, written in a language and character that would have puzzled any but a High Dutch commentator, or a learned decypherer of Egyptian obelisks, to understand. The sage Wouter took them one after the other, and having poised them in his hands, and attentively counted over the number of leaves, fell straightway into a very great doubt, and smoked for half an hour without saying a word ; at length, laying his finger beside his nose, and shutting his eyes for a moment, with the air of a man who has just caught a subtle idea by the tail, he slowly took his pipe from his mouth, puffed forth a column of tobacco-smoke, and, with marvellous gravity and solemnity, pronounced —that having carefully counted over the leaves and weighed the books, it was found that one was just as thick and heavy as the other; therefore, it was the final opinion of the Court that the accounts were equally balanced—therefore, Wandle should give Barent a receipt, and Barent should give Wandle a receipt."— *Knickerbocker's History of New York.*

No. 147. *Rodet.*   AWAITING AN AUDIENCE.

42.028

115 *H. Havemeyer*

IRVING (J. B.), N. A., dec'd. . . New York.

Born, 1826. Died, 1877.

450

THE END OF THE GAME.

30 x 25

116 *T. Van Volkenburgh*

RICO (M. D.) . . . . . Paris.

Pupil of Madrazo.
Medal, Exposition Universelle, 1878.
Legion of Honor, 1878.

900.

NEAR POISSY.

26 x 14

117 *E. a. Wicker*

WARD (Edgar M.), A. N. A. . . New York.

Pupil of Cabanel.

320

BRITTANY WASHERWOMAN.

32 x 35

118 *H. R. Bishop*

ZIEM (F.) . . . . Paris.

Medals, 1851, '52, '55.
Legion of Honor, 1857.
Officer of the Legion of Honor, 1878.

580

END OF THE GRAND CANAL.

32 x 20

44.283

No. 149   Wyant

October Landscape

44.283

119 *H. R. Bishop*

DE NITTIS (J.)   .   .   . Paris

200.

Pulpil of Gérome.
Medal, 1876. Exposition Universelle, 1878.
Legion of Honor, 1878.

THE PASSING TRAIN.

25 x 15

120 *Knoedler & Co*

CABANEL (Alexander)   .   . Paris.

920.

Pupil of Picot.
Medals, 1852 (E. U.) '55.
Prize of Rome, 1845.
Legion of Honor, 1855.
Member of the Institute of France, 1863.
Officer of the Legion of Honor, 1864.
Grand Medal of Honor, 1865, and (E. U.) 1867.
Commander of the Legion of Honor, 1878.
Grand Medal of Honor (E. U.) 1878.
Professor in the School of the Beaux Arts.

EVE AFTER THE EXPULSION FROM PARADISE.

37 x 29

R. H. Ewart.

121

HOMER (Winslow), N. A.   New York.

560.

SNAPPING THE WHIP.

35 x 22

45.963

45.963

122 *G. H. Peabody*

JAZET (P. L.) . . . . Paris.

Pupil of F. Barrias.

1.125 DIVIDING THE SPOILS.

28 x 23

123 *W. L. Strong*

BONHEUR (Juliette), Peyrol, . Paris.

Pupil of her sister.

375 A FLOCK OF TURKEYS.

39 x 22

124 *J Buell*

VERNON (A. L.) . . . . London.

Royal Academy, 1873.

200. THE GARDEN.

50 x 30

125 *Hart.*

DECAMPS (A. G.), dec'd. . . . Paris.

1.850. Pupil of Pujol.
Medals, 1831, '34.
Chevalier of the Legion of Honor, 1839.
Officer of the Legion of Honor, 1851.
Born, 1803. Died, 1860.

EASTERN SLAVE MARKET.

27 x 35

49.873

126   *C. a. Wickes*

HART (J. M.), N. A.   .   .   New York.

590.

CATTLE—INDIAN SUMMER.

48 x 35

127   *R. E. Moore*

GUY (S. J.), N. A.   .   .   New York.

A MOTHER'S SUPPLICATION.

600.

43 x 68

128   *R. Gieler*

VAN MARCKE (E.)   .   .   Paris.

Pupil of Troyon.
Medals, 1867, '69, '74.
Legion of Honor, 1872.
Medal, Exposition Universelle, 1878.

2900.

CATTLE—NEAR BORDEAUX.

58 x 41

129   *J. M. Benham*

ACHENBACH (Oswald) .   .   Düsseldorf.

Pupil of his brother.
Medals, 1859, '61, '63.
Legion of Honor, 1863.

525.

CONVENT OF ST. MONTREAL—PALERMO, SICILY.

64 x 44

5 H.128

54.128

130 *J. Buell*

KENSETT (J. F.), N. A., dec'd. . New York.

40 0. Born, 1818. Died, 1873.

THE WHITE MOUNTAINS—FROM NORTH CONWAY.

60 x 40

131 *G. G. Haven*

CLAYS (P. J.) . . . . Brussels.

2. 070 Medal, 1867 (E. U.)
Legion of Honor, 1875.
Chevalier of the Order of Leopold.
Medal, Exposition Universelle, 1878.

HARBOR—DUTCH COAST.

43 x 29

W. A. Wheelock

132

HERDMAN (Robert), R. S. A. . . Edinburgh.

FIRST CONFERENCE BETWEEN MARY STUART AND JOHN KNOX—HOLYROOD, 1561.

370. 52 x 36

" Whether it was by counsel of others, or by the Queen's own desire, we know not; but the Queen spake with John Knox, and had long reasoning with him, none being present except the Lord James. The sum of their reasoning was this. . . . 'Yea,' quoth she, 'but ye are not the Kirk that I will nourish. I will defend the Kirk of Rome. for I think *it* is the true Kirk of God.' '*Your* will,' quoth he, 'madam, is no reason.'"—*Knox's History of the Reformation in Scotland.*

57.025

57.02½

133 *Van Schaick*

WHITTREDGE (W.), N. A. . . New York.

28½.

TROUT STREAM—MILFORD, PA.

47 x 31

134 *Jno. Tondi*

SCHREYER (Ad.) . . . . Paris.

Medals, 1864, '65, '67 (E. U.)
Vienna Exposition, 1873.

2.42½

ARAB CARAVAN AT REST.

44 x 24

135 *E. H. Sarle*

DRUMMOND (Jas.), R. S. A. . . Edinburgh.

*ROUNDHEADS AND CAVALIERS—ROYALIST
PRISONERS.
HEADQUARTERS OF CROMWELL IN EDINBURGH.*

340.

48 x 36

The locality of this picture (destroyed in 1872) was called Dunbar's Close, Lawn Market. This Close got its name after the
battle of Dunbar (1650), when Cromwell marched to, and took
possession of Edinburgh. This Close he fixed upon as the headquarters of his army, and to this locality were brought prisoners,
both Cavaliers and Presbyterians, who were both at enmity with
the Cromwellian Roundheads. The bartizan in the middle of the
picture was that from which Cromwell received his troops in the
fields at the opposite side of the valley where the "New Town"
now stands. He could also see his fleet as it rode at anchor in
the Frith of Forth.

60.07½

60.073

136 *Van Sabaiok*

STEELL (Gourlay), R. S. A. . . Edinburgh.

Animal painter to the Queen in Scotland.

200 *SPRING IN THE HIGHLANDS.*

41 x 32

137 *H. R. Bishop*

VILLEGAS . . . . . Rome

Pupil of Fortuny.

460. *SPANISH DEVOTION.*

32 x 20

138 *J. G. Johnson*

GLAIZE (Léon) . . . . Paris/Phila

Pupil of Gérome.
Medals, 1864, '66, '68.
Legion of Honor, 1877.
Medal, Exposition Universelle, 1878.

800

THE CHINESE BAZAAR.

24 x 30

139 *J. B. Thornfield*

BROWN (J. G.), N. A. . . . New York.

"MY FAITH LOOKS UP TO THEE."

280. 20 x 29

61.513

61. 573

140 *Van Schaick*

GAUERMANN (F.), dec'd. . . Vienna.

Member of the Munich Academy.
Born, 1807. Died, 1862.

180. *CATTLE AND SHEEP.*

23 x 19

141 *Knoedler Co.*

RICHARDS (Wm. T.) . . Philadelphia.

PARADISE POINT, NEWPORT—SPRINGTIME.

300. 20 x 24

142 *B. B. Knight*

GUY (S. J.), N. A. . . . New York.

THE KNOT IN THE SKEIN.

350. 24 x 30

143 *H. O'Connor*

RÖTA (A.) . . . . Venice.

Medal, Exposition Universelle, 1878. *+2. W. 28.*

THE VETERANS.

No. 153. *Corot.*   EDGE OF A WOOD.

62,793

1,720

PALMAROLI (V.)   144   *H. L. Dousman*
                                         St. Louis

Pupil of F. Madrazo.
Prize of Rome, from Madrid, 1857.
Medals, 1862, '64, '71.
Medal, Paris, 1867.
Commander of the Order of Charles III.
Grand Cross of Marie-Victoire.
Grand Cross of Isabelle the Catholic.

THE PRETTY MODEL.

24 x 29

                     145   *R. G. Dun*

VAN MIERIS (W.), dec'd.   Leyden.

Born, 1662. Died, 1747.

1,100

TARQUIN AND LUCRETIA.

19¼ x 23½

From the Wolfe sale, 1863 ; and the Johnston sale, 1877.
Formerly in the collection of Thos. Hamlet, Esq., London.
"Wonderful detail in this exquisite and beautiful work of art."
Vide Smith's Catalogue Raisonné.

                     146   *Knoedler Bro.*

MADRAZO (R. de)   Paris.

1,320

Pupil of his father.
Legion of Honor, 1878.
Medal, Exposition Universelle, 1878.

A SPANISH DANCE.

16 x 25

No. 158. *Stevens.*   DISAPPOINTMENT.

66.943

R. H. Ewart

ROYBET (F.) . . . Paris.

790.

Pupil of
Medal, 1866.

AWAITING AN AUDIENCE.

18 x 24 *A. B. Butler*

148

WYANT (A. H.), N. A. . . . New York.

410.

OCTOBER LANDSCAPE.

24 x 18

149

RICO (M. D.) . . . Paris.

H. R. Bishop

470.

Pupil of Madrazo.
Medal, Exposition Universelle, 1878.
Legion of Honor, 1878.

ON THE SEINE.

17 x 12

150 *A. Cole*

SONNTAG (W. L.), N. A. . . . New York.

105.

SUNSET AT TIVOLI.

23 x 15

No. 159. Diaz.

In the Garden.

68.7/8

151   *Q. Q. Dyall*

ZIMMERMANN (R.) . . . . Munich.

210.

THE CONFESSIONAL.

24 x 16¼

R. H. Ewart

152

ZAMACOIS (E.), dec'd. . . . Paris.

625.

Pupil of E. Meissonier.
Medal, 1867.
Diploma to the memory of deceased artists.
Exposition Universelle, 1878.
Born, 1842.   Died, 1871.

MY CONCIERGE.

10 x 14

R. H. Ewart

153

COROT (J. B. C.), dec'd. . . . Paris.

260.

Pupil of V. Bertin.
Medals, 1838, '48, '55, '67 (E. U.)
Legion of Honor, 1846.
Officer of the Legion of Honor, 1867.
Diploma to the memory of deceased artists.
Exposition Universelle, 1878.
Born, 1796.   Died, 1875.

THE EDGE OF A WOOD.

16 x 20

No. 164. *Rossi.*   LADY.   TIME LOUIS XVI.

69.813.

VIRY (Paul)

154 *J. M. Benham* . Paris.

Pupil of Picot.

570.

THE MINIATURE—COSTUME OF LOUIS XIII.

14 x 12

155 *H. R. Bishop* . Rome.

MICHETTI (F. P.) .

Pupil of M. Morelli.

1.025

ITALIAN WATER-CARRIERS.

13 x 10

156 *R. H. Ewart.* . Paris.

TROYON (C.), dec'd.

Pupil of Rivereux.
Medals, 1838, '40, '46, '48, '55.
Legion of Honor, 1849.
Born, 1810. Died, 1865.

1.020

PASTURAGE—VALLEY OF THE TOUCQUE.

17 x 12

72.568

72.368

157 *J. Buell*

STEELL (David G.) . . . Edinburgh.

THE MITHERLESS LAMBIE.

150 19 × 14

158 *J. Buell*

STEVENS (Alfred) . . . Paris.

350 — Gold Medal at Brussels, 1851.
Paris, 1853, '55, '67 (E. U.)
Legion of Honor, 1863.
Officer of the Legion of Honor, 1867.
Commander of the Order of Leopold.
First-class Medal, Exposition Universelle, 1878.
Commander of the Legion of Honor, 1878.

DISAPPOINTMENT.

10 × 13

159 *R. H. Ewart*

DIAZ (N.), dec'd. . . Paris.

370. Medals, 1844, '46, '48.
Legion of Honor, 1851.
Diploma to the memory of deceased artists.
Exposition Universelle, 1878.
Born, 1807. Died, 1876.

IN THE GARDEN.

10 × 7

73.378

73.378

160 *H. R. Bishop* Paris.

GÉRÔME (J. L.) .

570.

Pupil of P. Delaroche.
Medals, 1847, '48, '55 (E. U.)
Legion of Honor, 1855.
Member of the Institute of France, 1865.
Honorary member R. A., London.
One of the Eight Grand Medals of Honor (E. U.), 1867.
Officer of the Legion of Honor, 1867.
Grand Medal of Honor, 1874.
Commander of the Legion of Honor, 1878.
Medal Sculpture (E. U.), 1878.
Grand Medal of Honor (E. U.), 1878.
Professor in the School of the Beaux Arts.

DIOGENES IN HIS TUB.

10 x 7

161 *J. D. Pruitt*

BOULANGER (G.) .   .   . Paris.

210.

Pupil of Paul Delaroche.
Prize of Rome, 1849.
Medals, 1857, '59, '63.
Legion of Honor, 1865.
Medal, Exposition Universelle, 1878.

CUPID'S WHISPER.

6⅜ x 10¼

74.158

162

COROT (J. B. C.), dec'd.

J. a. Stewart. Paris.

Pupil of V. Bertin.

410. Medals, 1838, '48, '55, '67 (E U.)
Legion of Honor, 1846.
Officer of the Legion of Honor, 1867.
Diploma to the memory of deceased artists.
Exposition Universelle, 1878.
Born, 1796. Died, 1875.

VILLAGE OF ST. CLOUD.

14 : 9

163

TROYON (Constant), dec'd. .

J. C. Runkle. Paris.

— Pupil of Rivereux.
720. Medals, 1838, '40, '46, '48, '55.
Legion of Honor, 1849.
Born, 1810. Died, 1865.

BOY WITH DONKEYS.

8½ x 6½

164

ROSSI (L.) . . .

S. J. Colgate. Paris.

Pupil of Fortuny.

470. *LADY—TIME LOUIS XVI.*

10 X 13

75.763

70. 763

A. R. Bishop

MEISSONIER (J. L. E.) 165 *N.* . . Paris.

2. 225

Pupil of Cogniet.
Medals, 1840, '41, '43, '48.
Legion of Honor, 1846.
Grand Medal of Honor (E. U.), 1855.
Officer of the Legion of Honor, 1856.
Member of the Institute of France, 1861.
Honorary Member of the R. A., London
One of the Eight Grand Medals of Honor (E. U), 1867.
Commander of the Legion of Honor, 1867.
Grand Medal of Honor (E. U.), 1878.

A HALT AT THE CABARET.

7½ x 6

77.988
6.239.04   Charges

71.748.96

www.ingramcontent.com/pod-product-compliance
Lightning Source LLC
Chambersburg PA
CBHW031442270326
41930CB00007B/830